My Pain BIRTHED My PURPOSE & My PASSION!

I SNAPPED OUT of IT!

QueenDeborah

ISBN 979-8-88616-775-7 (paperback)
ISBN 979-8-88616-777-1 (hardcover)
ISBN 979-8-88616-776-4 (digital)

Christian Faith Publishing
832 Park Avenue
Meadville, PA 16335
www.christianfaithpublishing.com

Printed in the United States of America

I am dedicating this book, to my Heavenly Father King Jesus! He has extended extreme and great mercy and abundance of grace to me! ***The Lord had shewed great mercy upon her; (Luke 1:58 KJV) I am her!***

This book is dedicated to the joy and the euphoria of finding one of my God-given purposes! As an author, I married my purpose and determined to reach all my greatest potentials! In the name of Jesus Christ! I believe there is much more in me, but God has truly blessed my beginning!

This book is dedicated to all in the world whoever has had, will have, or you are now in need of the great mercies of God! I am a witness that great mercy is available to all!

Rejoice not against me, O mine enemy: when I fall, I shall arise; when I sit in darkness, the Lord shall be a light unto me (Micah 7:8 KJV)

As you allow your pain to birth everything beautiful, and allow your purpose and passion to come forth now! Snap out of it! God has the power to allow you and I to rise and to stand!

Climax: "I snapped out of it; before I snapped!"

Introduction

Google definition(s)

*Pain: **Uncomfortable sensations in the body***
***Pain can range from annoying to debilitating. It may feel like a
sharp stab or a dull ache.***
***Purpose of pain: It allows the body to react and prevent further
tissue damage.***
***Purpose: The reason for which something is done or created or for
which something exists***
Passion: Strong and barely controllable emotion
***Snapped: Break or cause to break suddenly and completely, typi-
cally with a sharp cracking sound.***

Usually, the word *snapped* is used in a negative connotative; i.e.,
I snapped on him/her, I clowned them, I just went off on them, I
gave them a piece of my mind (Welp, a person keeps giving a piece
of their mind away; they will not have any left!) They gave all their
mind away, and they wonder why they are empty-headed! Ha, just
a little comedy! I love to laugh (a small insert). There is nothing like
laughing at yourself! You need to try it sometime!

Back to *snapped...* Another visual of snapped is a person's
mindset coming to a devastating breaking point, where they would
say they lost their mind. One would believe they had all that they
could stand and could not stand any more! Enough is enough! ***As
aunt Esther would say on Sanford and Son, "You old fish-eyed
fool!"*** She was at her snapping point. A twig being broken in half. Or
even a person being injured breaking a bone. When I had a snapping
moment, it was a place of, "You have gotten on my last nerve, and at

this point, I am going to let you know exactly how I feel!" (Oh, yes, I am still human; and yes, you may snap without cursing someone out!) How you may ask? It takes the Holy Ghost the Power of God to tame that tongue! *…but the tongue can no man tame; it is an unruly evil, full of deadly poison (James 3:8 KJV).* Again, it takes the power of GOD to tame the tongue.

There was a television show called *Snapped*. The series showed individuals who got to a certain point for one reason or another, and they got frustrated, stressed, depressed, oppressed; and watching a few of these series, it seemed like some of these individuals may have been demonically possessed. They got angered and snapped!

From viewing the Google definitions above, God brought a memory to mind; I do not recall how old I was at the time, but certainly, it was in my adolescent years. My mother had a tall old iron-steel garage in the back of the house. I was skateboarding, and I hit that old garage several times along with many of my other siblings. One day, that old garage door hinged snapped and fell on my back from my neck down. I should have been dead or paralyzed! But God gave me a praying mother who not only talked what she believed but also lived that thang, and God responded to her on my behalf! I never had to use a wheelchair or anything!

This book is to help you recall the many times you may have overlooked those moments and painful memories that seemed to be pure dismay, but PURPOSE and true PASSION were birthed! This book is to let you know that no matter what you may have deemed, calculated, or stated, you missed opportunities from PAIN! You may truly declare that by the GRACES and MERCIES of God, a lot more was BIRTHED, and it's called PURPOSE and PASSION! So go ahead and SNAP OUT of IT!

Pit to PURPOSE: God Has Purpose for your
PAIN, a Reason for Your Struggle, and Reward
for Your Faithfulness. (Krissy Scott)

Reflections

My late pastor Bishop Dr. Michael Ford Sr. preached a sermon, "I Admit It, I Did It, But I Quit!" Before completing my first book, TURNING FROM… TURNING TO… MY TURNING POINT the thought came to me; I also SNAPPED OUT OF IT! My TURNING POINT helped me to do just that, SNAP OUT OF IT! My SNAPPING OUT OF IT was the merry-go-round of allowing myself to be in ungodly, unhealthy, toxic, the roller coaster ride of relationships that GOD Himself did not want me in and to understand that these egotistical and narcissistic men did not deserve a GODLY, ambitious, tenacious, audacious, and vivacious woman like me! What is your IT that you need to SNAP OUT of?

The first place SNAPPING OUT OF IT must take place is in the mind. If you do not have a made up mind to do better, be better, and make better choices, you'll get the same results over and over again! I don't know about you, but after reaching my ultimate TURNING POINT, I can't help but SNAP OUT of the atrocious behavior and ways that I allowed myself to pattern for years.

Let this mind be in you, which was also
in Christ Jesus. (Philippians 2:5 KJV)

A lot of times when pain is felt or has surfaced to the brain that something is not right, it feels dreadful, uneasy, debilitating, demobilizing, and uncertain! There are times when pain hits, and it is unexpected! For some, pain is hitting your hand with a hammer, hitting your funny bone, cutting your finger cleaning fish or cooking, or stepping out of bed walking to the bathroom, and you happened to kick or stump your toe so unexpectedly! Somebody, say, "OUCH!"

Then there are times when pain could be expected. An example is looking forward to the delivery date of a pregnancy, and if no one has mentioned it to you; yes, there is some pain. I know some females who gave birth naturally and quickly. I say kudos to you; I was not privileged! Ha! A person who crossed the street without looking both ways is asking for pain or even death. Individuals running red lights and taking that risk can cause pain not only for them but also for others involved!

Prior to God birthing and allowing me to marry my purpose and becoming an author and writing my first book, an individual stated to me, "I kinah like pain!" My response was, "Ugh, please do not tell that to anyone else, let alone everybody!" She is probably one in a few who would honestly admit that they like pain! Um, go check with a doctor. (LOL if you like it, I love it! Be you, do you!)

Any time I had experienced pain expected or unexpected, it did not feel good, and there were times I hated that feeling! How about you?

And we know that all things work together
for the good to them that love God and
to them who are the called according
to his purpose. (Romans 8:28 KJV)

MY PAIN BIRTHED MY PURPOSE & MY PASSION!

THE SHIFT

In the twenty-one years of journaling, I would have never dreamed or thought about becoming an author or even writing books, and that the time would be now! God certainly turned what seemed to be the worst of times that BIRTHED my PURPOSE and allowed the sun to shine to surface much PASSION, therefore bringing about the best of times and something amazing!

...:but let them that love him be as the
sun when he goeth forth in his might.
(Judges 5:31 KJV)

When I taught elementary school as a preferred substitute teacher in 2009, the librarian was retiring, and she stated, "Queen, I have a gift for you. It was a journal!"

I told her I had been journaling for over ten years at the time since I was pregnant with my daughter.

She stated, "This journal is for the books that you will be writing to use for reflections!"

Wow, that was 2009! Who would have known twelve years later in 2021 that I would fulfill that prophecy! The librarian did not know she was prophesying to me, and by George, I too did not see it as a prophecy, speaking for what was to come!

Wow! I'm telling you, God can use anybody to speak life into what HE has in store for the future, which we would call DESTINY and/or our PURPOSE! I wish I could find her and let her know that a PURPOSE has been BIRTHED and that she spoke of being an author over my life! I truly did not know or ever thought about becoming an author, let alone writing books! Then on top of that, writing two books! But a scripture comes to mind, *For my thoughts are not your thoughts, neither are your ways my ways, saith the Lord (Isaiah 55:8 KJV).*

It was earlier in the year 2021 when God blessed me to SNAP OUT of my foolishness and everything opposing His will. I was watching **R. C. Blake's ministry series.** I do not recall which one, and he stated, *"That your gift/entrepreneurship is in your house."* I literally started looking around my house and asking God what is my gift/entrepreneurship. He took his reference from **II Kings 4:1–7** for the widow to gather containers", fill them up with oil, and to live on the rest! And not many days, hence God told me to write my first book, *TURNING FROM… TURNING TO… MY TURNING POINT!* Wow! You cannot tell me that God cannot take what seems to be a horrible or devastating situation and make or birth something beautiful out of it! *He hath made every thing beautiful in his time… (Ecclesiastes 3:11 KJV).* I have stepped into what I believe God has called "My TIME!"

> *Thou shalt arise, and have mercy upon*
> *Zion: for the time to favour her, the set*
> *time, is come. (Psalm 102:13 KJV)*

Reflect on your life in that place(s) of pain. How did you handle it? Did the circumstance overwhelm you? Did you feel that you were drowning, or did you seek God and quote His word, *I shall not die, but live… (Psalm 118:17 KJV).* It is okay. Only you and Jesus need to know how you felt! I know I felt at times that I was going to drown and burn up, but God brought His Word to me.

> *When thou passest through the waters, I*
> *will be with thee; and through the rivers*
> *they shall not overflow thee: when you*
> *walk through the fire you shall not burned*
> *neither shall flame kindle upon you.*
> *(Isaiah 43:2 KJV)*

What we do in that time of pain impacts everything within that present moment and future! If we allow that moment of pain to educate and empower us, there is an opportunity of birthing something even greater that's equivocated and called Purpose!

> *A woman when she is travail hath sorrow*
> *because her hour is come; but as soon as*
> *she delivered of the child, she remembered*
> *no more anguish, for joy that a man is*
> *born into the world. (John 16:21 KJV)*

The scripture above referenced about when a woman is giving birth at that moment it is extremely painful! (We may thank Eve for this! She ate the forbidden fruit that God told her not to! But that is another book by itself!) For some women, their delivery may have been a quick birth in seconds or minutes; some birthed in hours, and some may have been in labor for a day or longer. But joy came once that bundle of joy came forth!

MY PAIN BIRTHED MY PURPOSE & MY PASSION!

Destiny aka Purpose

I am a mother of two wonderful children: my beautiful daughter named Destiny and my handsome son named Darius. My children and I have grown through a lot together. I got married at the young age of twenty as a virgin and had my daughter at the age of twenty-one. What should have been an exciting time for me was extremely painful. That is why I named my daughter Destiny because despite the pain and anguish I dealt with, she was purposed to be here and to become something great in this world! I was not perfect, but I did do things the way my mother taught me. She raised me to wait until marriage to have sex so that I would not become a single mother. But the fact of getting married, the pain of being married, and living single while married felt so detrimental!

At times I felt why in the world did I wait on what seemed to be a sexual pleasure to be treated so horribly! If you recall from my first book, I stated how God always warned me not to deal or be in relationships because His hand of Mercy, Grace, and Favor is on my life for the best! Welp, there goes that human nature that gets us in a heap and whirlwind of trouble! But again, out of pain, God knows how to birth something beautiful; and as you read on, you will find out my daughter Destiny was born! God told me prior to marrying at the young age of twenty when I prayed about marrying my kids' father, His will was, "Stay separate!"

I broke things off for two years, and then this joker or clown, as I would call mirages or imitations, came back around! I asked someone dear to me his opinion! Hmm! I did not go back to God in prayer but asked an individual, and they questioned whether God would tell me what I believe God told me? I listened to this individual and got married young. Not listening to my mother, she said,

"

"He is going to hurt you many days!" (referencing my ex-husband). My marriage turned out to be everything GOD and my mother had spoken! Even though we were married, we had nothing together, and his whole ammo when married and divorced was to hurt me and our children. Was I perfect? No! But when I say this was a learning experience, GOD showed Himself Consistent, Faithful, and Loyal to me!

I know how it was for me to observe my mother being married but living single. She raised eleven boys and four girls—the majority of the time by herself! My father was emotionally and, at times, physically abusive. I knew I did not want to travel down that road and stay there. My ex had pushed me down on the bed, hit me with a belt, and would act highly aggressive in behavior; and he took me for this young naïve church girl, green as some would say. Yes, I would raise both of my hands and say I was extremely green and naive! That was me! I never told my eleven brothers how he treated me because I did not want them to be mad at him and the possible chaos that could come with telling them of all the hell I was enduring!

But may I say I learned quickly not to allow any person to abuse me that way, form, or fashion! My mother never allowed any of my eleven brothers to be physical or abusive toward me! How dare I allow this joker or clown? When I started thinking about ways that I had to protect my kids and myself, I knew things had to change! Even if that meant me leaving for good! We had separated so many times because I did not desire to be a single mom, but nothing or no one is worth your life or freedom!

One day before I thought I would SNAP, I went to McDonald's and sat at the table. I did the famous T-chart I told you all about on page ten in my first book. The thing we do and tried to convince ourselves to stay in these crazy, hideous, and hostile relationships. I sat at McDonald's and wrote down the pros and cons of staying in this marriage. The only pro was that I did not want to be a single mother. I did not want my children to experience what I had all the years of my life—single parenting. Welp, when we do not OBEY GOD, and if He does not allow His mercy and grace to kick in, what do we get? At that moment and in that time, it feels like pure hell and anguish of soul! But God! ***But God, who is rich in mercy, for his great love wherewith he loved us (Ephesians 2:4 KJV).***

***You are free to choose, but you are
not free from the consequences
of your choice (Zig Ziglar)***

I married the wrong person! How many know and would honestly admit from your experience? Yes, I did too! He was so mentally, emotionally, and spiritually abusive. I thank God my mother raised me in church to know God's Word for myself because the church he attended was just as repulsive, abusive, manipulating, controlling, and to sum it up, diabolical! It would be another book if I would write about the hell that marrying the wrong person could bring, but again, it still birthed purpose; and down the road, passion has resurfaced!

Yes, there is church hurt and abuse, but people are people wherever you go. But it is important to know God for yourself! I accepted God in my life at the age of thirteen, and that changed my whole path of destiny! How adventurous God has made me; He knew I needed to be in church at a young age. However, it is sad in the arena that people call themselves church folk and Christians in public, and they use Bible verses to manipulate, control, demonize, and abuse their mates and/or people.

MY PAIN BIRTHED MY PURPOSE & MY PASSION!

Facing the Noise

I heard Bishop T. D. Jakes say, "People
are public success but private failures!"

In front of crowds, people look the part of being valued and esteemed; but in the privacy of their homes and behind closed doors, they are failures in communication, romance, unity, and have a Jekyll and Hyde mentality! They do not know how to relate to their mates or children; they have no relationship but desired to be center of attention to others!

This goes for males and females in the church. I have seen men and women in the church use Bible verses to manipulate their wives and husbands to do what they wanted them to do! I know there are people out there, male and female, who desire to be loved, loyal, and true to GOD; but we do not have to use the name of GOD to abuse or manipulate others.

When you are giving BIRTH, a couple of things happen: The doctors monitor the moms' and babies' heart rate, blood pressure, and the positioning of the baby, especially once the baby is birthed. Are there any blood clots, additional pain, fever, blood pressure, or hemorrhoids? Did the baby cry? And more so now, Does the mom suffer from postpartum depression?

I was six months pregnant with my daughter DESTINY, and I was not showing. My doctor who was out of state where I was married and living at the time was highly concerned with my health and the place to which I would give BIRTH. I had to return to Kentucky to birth my daughter DESTINY. (The place you are in to give BIRTH is incredibly important.) I was not gaining weight and being in an abusive marriage, and out of state was not the place to be BIRTHING DESTINY!

Upon having DESTINY there were several times I asked my mom to hold and keep her! When I had her, she was so light, complicated with silver-gray eyes! Wow, I birthed this beautiful angel with a head full of hair—just gorgeous!

In 1999, the talk of postpartum depression was not as expressed as it is now, and I did not know why I was not as clingy to my daughter as I should have been. PAIN may have you acting in all types of ways and with the wrong ones. But not having my husband by my side at the time of her birth only for both of us to be spited by him; then to have waited to do things the right way, all types of emotions and depression that I did not know at the time set in. I was going to name my daughter Dasha', Diamond, or DESTINY. I had so many signs around me, so DESTINY it is! I still call her my SUNSHINE because, in my darkest hour, GOD gave me light.

Despite the pain, postpartum depression, and disappointment my children and I had to grow through in that seven-year marriage, I still BIRTHED DESTINY aka PURPOSE!

When I was pregnant with my daughter, Destiny, while going through anger, frustration, disappointment, and all type of emotions. From being abused emotionally, spiritually, and attempts of physical abuse, the devil told me to commit suicide and to swallow all my prenatal pills! God Almighty immediately spoke to me and said, "You do that you will immediately go to hell!" I SNAPPED OUT of that thought! I was like no sir! ***...everlasting fire, prepared for the devil and his angels: (Matthew 25:41)***. So if God Almighty did not help me snap out of it, that would have sealed not only my fate but my unborn child at the time! God helped me to snap out of it! Thank you, Father God, King Jesus!

***God has purpose for your pain, a
reason for your struggle and a reward
for your faithfulness. Don't give up.
(MagiQuotes added the "Don't give
up" from Krissy Scott quote)***

MY PAIN BIRTHED MY PURPOSE & MY PASSION!

REBUILDING OF ONESELF

When a person needs a doctor for a broken foot, toe, arm, back, or hand, would it make sense to try to doctor oneself? I think common sense would say no! So many people have been hurt attending church or by people in the church and have endured such hurt in the church where churches should have been seen as a hospital to treat and nourish hurt people to health! When church hurt happens, that is the devil using people in a diabolical way to stop a person's growth both naturally and spiritually!

People say, "Connect to a higher power, connect to something, reach beyond yourself when you need healing, especially within." Welp, I know NO other HIGHER POWER but KING JESUS GOD HIMSELF.

For what if some did not believe?
shall their unbelief make the faith of
God without effect? (Romans 3:3)

Let every soul be subject unto the
higher powers. For there is no power
but of God: the powers that be are
ordained of God. (Romans 13:1)

GOD IS THE HIGHER POWER! So many people have decided not to ever go to church again because of people who have caused them PAIN. Ugh, but just think. You get hurt at work (someone talks crazy), a club (a drink gets wasted on you, and you get into a fight), a store (someone takes your parking space), road rage (someone gives you the middle finger), and other venues of gatherings, but that does not stop you from going to that site or destination! Even people pulling a Madea on you, pulling in the parking space that you had your blinker on to turn into. UGH! Now that can set someone off! That happened to me twice in the month of November 2021, but GOD helped me keep my cool! But I was bothered! But it did not stop me from going into the store and shopping. I found another parking space and went into the store anyway!

So do not let anyone keep you from going to church; go into church and get what you need and go home! Some of the best advice I could have received. People are not going home for dinner or to a movie with you unless you invite them.

Going or being hurt in the church is no different from going to the stores, malls, work, or concerts; wherever people are, you may face hurt, but that doesn't stop you from going or attending! So go to church and get over it like you would anywhere else! Again, people are people, and even the devil is at church.

I know thy works, and where thou dwellest, even where Satan's seat is… (Revelations 2:13 KJV)

Not forsaking the assembling of ourselves together, as the manner of some is; but exhorting one another: and so much the more, as ye see the day approaching. (Hebrews 10:25 KJV)

What day is approaching? The coming of the LORD JESUS CHRIST, either by RAPTURE for the entire church or just calling people by name individually! We need GOD! HE is the only one who can rebuild us, and if anything needs to be broken off, HE will not hurt us; it is only for our making!

Hath not the potter power over the clay, of the same lump to make one vessel unto honour, and another unto dishonour? (Romans 9:21 KJV)

...For without me ye can do nothing. (John 15:5)

What does not kill you makes you STRONGER! (Friedrich Nietzsche, a nineteenth-century German philosopher)

Moving On

When pain occurs in the body, the white blood cells immediately go to give aid for the preservation of what may be preserved. When GOD sustains us through painful situations, it is an opportunity for rebirth if we allow it.

How may you ask? How do I rebuild after such pain? Especially depending on the level of the pain that occurred. One of my favorite Psalm in the Bible is Psalm 139.

O LORD, thou hast searched me, and know me. Thou knowest my downsitting and mine uprising, thou understandest my thought afar off. Thou compassest my path and my lying down, and art acquainted with all my ways. For there is not a word in my tongue, but lo, O LORD, thou knowest it altogether. Thou hast beset me behind and before and laid thine hand upon me. Such knowledge is too wonderful for me; it is high, I cannot attain unto it. Whither shall I go from thy spirit? or whither shall I flee from thy presence? If I ascend up into heaven, thou art there: if I make my bed in hell, behold, thou art there. If I take the wings of the morning, and dwell in the uttermost parts of the sea; Even there shall thy hand lead me, and thy right hand shall hold me. If I say, Surely the darkness shall cover me; even the night shall be light about me. Yea, the darkness, and the light are both alike to thee. For thou hast possessed my riens: thou hast covered me in my mother's womb. I will praise thee; for I am fearfully and wonderfully made: marvellous are thy works; and that my soul knoweth right well. My substance was not hid from thee, when I was made in secret, and curiously wrought in the lowest parts of the earth. Thine eyes did see my substance, yet being unperfect; and in thy book all my members were written, which in continuance were fashioned, when as yet there was none of them. How precious also are thy thoughts unto me O God! how great is the sum of them! If I should count them, they are more in number than the sand: when I awake, I am still with thee. Surely thou wilt slay the wicked, O God: depart from me therefore, ye bloody men. For they speak against thee wickedly, and thine enemies take thy name in vain. Do not I hate them, O LORD that hate thee? and am not I grieved with those that rise up against thee? I hate them with perfect hatred: I count them mine enemies. Search me, O God, and know my heart: try me, and know my thoughts: And see if there be any wicked way in me, and lead me in the way everlasting. (Psalm 139:1–24 KJV)

Only the Creator who created us can give us the HEALING and TURNING POINT that is needed! Before writing this second book, God gave me an epiphany (***GOD gave me this epiphany on March 3, 2021), "Because GOD'S LOVE is enough to comfort and to HEAL; HIS LOVE is enough to keep me and to BE STILL!"***

Ask GOD to help you turn to HIM, and everything you tell yourself in this moment in time may feel like an eternity and is paramount! But be assured that this too shall pass! I am a witness! You must be comfortable and ask GOD to help you to be confident to speak life over yourself.

> *I shall not die, but live, and declare*
> *the works of the LORD.*
> *(Psalm 118:17)*

> *Death and life are in the power of the*
> *tongue: and they that live it shall eat*
> *the fruit thereof. (Proverbs 18:21)*

YES, what you say about yourself to yourself is everything! YOU have already been beaten down externally; you cannot afford to internally gouge yourself! You got to know what you need when you need it! Just make sure what you are needing is that of promoting personal health and nothing of self-injury. Also, go back and reread my first book, *Turning from… Turning to… My Turning Point!* Chapter 5 "Building Up Yourselves (Knowing Who We Are)" page forty speaks on the "I am" factors as God titles this! Speak well over yourself as you are moving on!

An epiphany God gave me on August 7, 2022 was "When you're spiritually okay, you'll be mentally okay. When you're mentally okay, you'll be emotionally okay. When you're emotionally okay, you'll be physically okay. When you're physically okay, you'll be financially okay because you'll be sound and stable to enjoy it all!"

TIMES

To every thing there is a season, and a time to every purpose under the heaven: A time to be born, and a time to die; a time to plant, and a time to pluck up that which is planted; A time to kill, and a time to heal; a time to break down, and a time to build up; A time to weep, and a time to laugh; a time to mourn, and a time to dance; A time to cast away stones, and a time to gather stones together; a time to embrace, and a time to refrain from embracing; A time to get, and a time to lose; a time to keep, and a time to cast away; A time to rend, and a time to sew; a time to keep silence, and a time to speak; A time to love, and a time to hate; a time of war, and a time of peace. 11 He hath made every thing beautiful in his time. (Ecclesiastes 3:1–8 and v. 11 KJV)

Wow! GOD's Word is so deep! Those words above speak volumes! GOD'S word covers a cycle in time when life will demand a response and the response and or choice that is rendered will manifest results good or bad.

THE GOOGLE definition of TIME is (1) "the indefinite continued progress of existence and events in the past, present, and future regarded as a whole."

God, being God, He controls TIME! He operates outside the sphere of time and therefore cannot be controlled by our small minds of what time is and when time should be!

There are times when being alone and doing self-evaluation is everything! Take your time and how ever long that is needed! But that is the issue. We rush the process of healing and/or take our time for whatever it may be. We try to hurry God! An ole school church song, ***"You can't hurry GOD you just have to wait!"*** It is the waiting that gets us, the very entity of why we rush! We rush traffic, we rush our kids if they are not developing or growing as quickly as we think they should, and shoot, we try to rush the pastor's sermons! In church, people will say a lot of *amens* or sit quietly so the preacher or pastor could end their sermon quickly so we could do what we wanted to do afterward. We are at times in a HURRY! May you raise your hand and say, "Guilty!" HA! We all should be smiling right there! We know what we do!

If you are needing additional company during those hard moments, that is okay; everyone is different. I know an individual who told me she likes pain. Umm, I would not tell too many people that! I know it has been said that if you cannot handle your own company or spend time alone, you may not be ready for anything else; but again, seek God and be wise for what is good for you! I do believe it is wise not to rush into another relationship if you are coming out of an abusive one so that those same mistakes are not repeated!

> ***The definition of insanity is "doing the same thing and expecting a different result."***

We need to take our time so that those same mistakes are not repeated! One group of people that should be avoided are the ones that would tell you or mock you, "That is what you get, I told you so, I told you if you do that then this would happen, this is the cause from your effect!" STOP just STOP...welp Einstein it does not take a novice to realize when someone makes a minor or major mistake especially when it is visible. A person gets pregnant, a divorce, a relationship failed, a person's hair falls out; this is your time to retreat for your own sanity. Position yourself around people who will help you level up mentally! You pull your mind out of the pain, your actions will respond to what you tell your mind!

Always remember and I know this for certain; this thought GOD ALMIGHTY gave me *"What may seem like the worst of times can BIRTH the best of times even that of PURPOSE!"* You must be still and let GOD lead and guide you!

> *Be still, and know that I am God: I will*
> *be exalted among the heathen, I will be*
> *exalted in the earth. (Psalm 46:10 KJV)*

> *What people say or think of you has very little*
> *to do with what you say or think of yourself*
> *from within! WOW, thank you, FATHER GOD!*
> *Epiphany GOD gave me on April 17, 2021.*
> *That when you do not know who you*
> *are within and operate from that place,*
> *you'll compromise and negotiate without!*
> *(My first book, TURNING FROM... TURNING*
> *TO... MY TURNING POINT! p. 14)*

MY PAIN BIRTHED MY PURPOSE & MY PASSION!

Why Must Pain Be the Biggest but Best Teacher

From our infant stages, we learn *dos* and *don'ts* from our parents! Do not touch hot skillets. Do not touch hot irons or stoves. Do not play with sockets. Do not lay or stick anything in the sockets. Look both ways before crossing the streets. Do not play with matches or fire. Do not have sex before marriage; there are too many sexually transmitted diseases. You do not want to have babies all over the place with different people, and so forth.

Why were we taught not to do these things? It's because our parents knew that if we did such things, there could be lasting consequences! But how many of us are guilty of doing things that we know we should not have done as kids and even now as adults?

> *Train up a child in the way he should*
> *go: And when he is old, he will not*
> *depart from it. (Proverbs 22:6 KJV)*

For those of us raised in church, especially in the Apostolic Pentecostal Faith, we should know the above scripture oh-too well! The verse references that no matter how old we are, the teachings we get from our birth and especially of the Word of God have lasting impressions that will never leave us! That still, small voice will always come to you: Do not do that, you know better, your mother said, didn't your pastor say, and God Himself will speak.

> ***Can a man take fire in his bosom and his
> clothes not be burned? (Proverbs 6:27 KJV)***

Remember even as adults, many of us have had to relearn don't play with fire! Yeah, being in that God-forsaken relationship, being with the wrong one, may cost you everything if God does not have mercy! Some of us have touched hot stoves, skillets, and pots; and some get distracted and forgot to look both ways before crossing the road.

> ***You are free to choose, but you are
> not free from the consequences of
> your choice. (Zig Ziglar)***

In life, we have the scars from being burned physically, emotionally, sexually, spiritually, mentally, and financially! I guarantee those words of wisdom that were told to us, if we had listened, we could have avoided the pitfalls that almost engulfed and could have drowned us, but God.

Some people think that because they are considered three times seven, they no longer must listen to anyone, or any of the wholesome teachings no longer exist, only to end up damaged! It is something about being scarred you will never forget it! But this book has been written with the inspiration of God to let you know all is not lost! That pain with God's help can still BIRTH your PURPOSE gives much PASSION, and it is not too late! It's because God has allowed and puts breath in our bodies. Somebody, say, "YES, LORD! Thank you, KING JESUS!"

Resilience

> *If it had not been the Lord who was on our side, now Israel say; If it had not been the Lord who was on our side, when me rose up against us: Then they had swallowed us up quick, when their wrath was kindled against us: Then the waters had overwhelmed us, the stream had gone over our soul: Then the proud waters had gone over our soul. Blessed be the Lord, who hath given us as a prey to their teeth. Our soul is escaped as a bird out of the snare of the fowlers: the snare is broken, and we are escaped. Our help is in the name of the Lord, who made heaven and earth. (Psalm 124:1–8)*

If it had not been for the Lord King Jesus on my side, I am not sure where I would be! Some people may think that they are hurting you when they walk away, reject, or shun you; but little do they know they just helped you at the fork in the road to make their exit debut! The decision that you knew had to take place sooner than later! God gives us that sense to know when something is not going to last or if it is not good for us! We would like for it to last, but it is a hindrance to our destiny aka Purpose! This year, on October 15, 2021, God told me, "I had mercy on you!" Wow! I screamed and cried just to know God Almighty and all-powerful allowed mercy to set in upon little ole me!

I thank God for the resilience He has placed on the inside of me to keep it movin'! There have been several times I just wanted to lay in bed, mope, and just rehearse in my mind the bamboozle that just happened! There were times I just wanted to walk away and give up, but GOD would not let me! My kids were my motivation when I thought all was lost, but GOD had already told me, "INTUITIVE, and it's NOT OVER!" GOD cannot lie! When I think of resilience, I think of the forty-six-inch Bozo Bop Bag; if you kick or hit it, it bounces right back! I thank GOD for the GRACE and MERCY to bounce back!

I must admit, GOD used my kids at my lowest to be my saving grace! I never talked about depression personally. I heard of people being or feeling depressed, but to have experienced it myself before 2011, I did not know what that was! I had just been wrongfully terminated from a job, a profession that I highly loved and enjoyed! Welp, depression hit me. I was lying in bed and just finished eating lots and lots of candies and junk foods. My eleven-year-old daughter, DESTINY, came to me and said, "Mom, Darius and I do not like how you've been acting!" I apologized to my daughter, and the only thing I could do was fall on my face to GOD in my basement, pleading for HIS MERCY! I knew I had to SNAP OUT of IT for my kids!

My late pastor Bishop Dr. Michael E. Ford Sr. used to say, "The devil wanted to kill me, but GOD would not let me die!" Why would GOD not let me die? It's because HE knew HE had the ability to let my PAIN BIRTH my PURPOSE and bring about much PASSION!

MY PAIN BIRTHED MY PURPOSE & MY PASSION!

WHY MUST WE BE SO CURIOUS

Why must curiosity kill the cat. (Ben Jonson)

Too many of us are too curious! We stay in relationships or situations curious to find out if we could twist or redefine in some way, shape, or form. We think we can fix or change people and things all at the same time! While we are forgetting the longer we are curious and inadvertently trying to change someone or something, we are the ones who need to be changed!

If we do not have the ability to change or fix ourselves, what makes us so curious to think that if we hold on to this person, place, or thing we may get a different result?

When people show you who they are,
believe them. (Maya Angelou)

Maya Angelou's quote above may be a hard pill for some people to swallow. I know it has been for me. We always want to be kind and merciful to people and then hope things could be mended if it is a family member, church member, coworker, or a person we have a relationship with. We try to look past their issues, but if the situation or relationship is not healthy and beneficial, you/we have to do the next best thing!

Unfortunately, many of us had to find out the hard and painful way. Some people get in a relationship, thinking this situation or individual may change after marriage or after more financial investments are made. If they do all the sex moves that were desired of them, then a person may choose them. No, pay attention early! Why must curiosity kill the cat? Why must curiosity kill so many people?

Curiosity has shattered hearts, has broken down minds, spirits, and has tried to kill dreams and hope! But believe me, PAIN can BIRTH your PURPOSE! Look to JESUS!

> *Looking unto Jesus the author*
> *and finisher of our faith.*
> *(Hebrews 12:2 KJV)*

JESUS can help you and give you the faith that is needed! Again, a lot of people refuse to accept that lust of the flesh is never satisfied! Eventually a person may make a person feel that being in a relationship without the commitment of marriage and unlimited sex should be enough. WRONG! I heard ***Pastor R. C. Blakes say in a podcast that a man will pay for rent/mortgage, a car note, but he will not pay for you. He wants you to settle to be a girlfriend, but not a wife!***

> *And GOD said unto Noah, The end*
> *of all flesh is come before me; for the*
> *earth is filled with violence through*
> *them; and behold, I will destroy them*
> *with the earth. (Genesis 6.13 KJV)*

> *Love not the world, neither the things that are*
> *in the world... For all that is in the world,*
> *the lust of the flesh, and the lust of the eyes,*
> *and the pride of life, is not of the Father, but*
> *is of the world. And the world passeth away*
> *and the lust thereof: (1 John 2.15–17 KJV)*

We are now in the time of the verse above, where GOD tells Noah that the end of all flesh is coming! It is curiosity that holds a person to see how long one may endure such tremendous pain mentally, emotionally, some physically, sexually, spiritually, and financially before they snapped and reached that breaking point!

As human beings, we are always so curious. That is why when people try one thing, they are so eager to try the next big thing whether it is drugs, alcohol, or sex moves; it's the curiosity that kills the cat! I visualize curiosity as persons who are focused on what's in front of them, and they have tunnel vision or even have a horse's bridle vision. They do not see the things that may occur in the peripheral visions. We only see what we want to see! We want what we want when we want it! Have you ever seen someone sitting like they are in a trance or hypnotized? It is not until a person snapped their finger or vehemently called their name that they SNAPPED out of it!

What causes a person to snap out of it? Usually, it is caused by something dramatic or traumatic that happened and makes a person stop, think, and consider! A person considered things after death, child concerns, loss of job, divorce, scandal exposed, or even a world catastrophe!

God Has a Way

God has a way to make PAIN birth PURPOSE! One is the prayer of JABEZ!

> *...and his mother called his name Jabez,*
> *saying, Because I bare him with sorrow. And*
> *Jabez called on the God of Israel, saying,*
> *Oh that thou wouldest bless me indeed, and*
> *enlarge my coast, and that thine hand might*
> *be with me, and that thou wouldest keep me*
> *from evil, that it may not grieve me! And*
> *God granted him that which he requested.*
> *(I Chronicles 4:9–10 KJV)*

Jabez said, "I know what my mother may have declared over me because of her own personal pain, but I am not what my mother named me." See, he reached for GOD who created him from his mother's womb. He was like GOD. I do not know the pain his mother has endured spiritually, mentally, emotionally, physically, or even sexually before his arrival; but he was like GOD. I am not that.

This shows us that despite what our parents may have done and even named us, if it is not favorable, look to GOD the one who holds all favor! He granted Jabez his request. Jabez humbled himself before GOD ALMIGHTY! A lot of our problem is that we are not humble, and we do not allow GOD to be GOD! Let us take a second and ask GOD to forgive us to help us to be humble before HIM and help us to let

Him be GOD! We got to accept GOD is the only one who can change us or our situations! HE HAS ALL POWER!

And Jesus came and spake unto them,
saying, All power is given unto me in heaven
and in earth. (Matthew 28:18 KJV)

It is not enough to say GOD is Mighty
HE is ALMIGHTY, it is not enough to say
HE is Powerful, HE is All-Powerful! (An
epiphany GOD gave me on December 26,
2021, the last Sunday of the year)

Jabez's name meant sorrow/pain, but he knew GOD had the ability and power to reverse the curse that was pronounced over his life! Jabez believed GOD is ALMIGHTY and ALL-POWERFUL! Have you ever crossed paths with people that you grew up with? They were the ones who tried to bully you, talked about you, labeled you, put you down, and even looked down on you. You see them five, ten, or even twenty years later in life, and they look worn out, stuck, or may even be in the same place for years without any change or growth. Not that you are comparing yourself, but your observation is not blurred.

Your PAINS in life have BIRTHED PURPOSE and catapulted you to the next level! GOD has a way of birthing us through the PAIN that will BIRTH our PURPOSE. Who would have known that the PAIN of breaking off a relationship would have BIRTHED me into becoming an author! But yes, that PAIN did! And becoming an author is only the beginning!

What GOD is getting ready to do in my life is BIGGER than my eyes can see and GREATER than I can hold in my hand! **I found myself, my PURPOSE, and MY PASSION when I DROPPED HIM! Let me say that again, I FOUND MYSELF, MY PURPOSE, and MY PASSION when I DROPPED HIM!** Some of y'all need to DROP some people off! Imagine yourself being a bus driver, drop those clowns off at an arena, Greyhound bus station, park, or somewhere. Just drop them out of your life! THEY are extra weights of unnecessary baggage and pounds! You will feel so much lighter with them out of your life! That little extra nugget was free! Ha! LOL, yessss! Yes, get glad about it! I AM!!!!!!!!

> *...let us lay aside every weight, and the sin which doth so easily beset us, let us run with patience the race that is set before us. (Hebrews 12:1 KJV)*

> *If you can't figure out your purpose, figure out your passion. For your passion will lead you right into your purpose. (Bishop T. D. Jakes)*

Passion

My mother raised me to love, serve, and respect GOD! Growing up, I had such a PASSION and hunger for GOD. I would pray for hours growing up and memorize chapters of the Bible and several Bible verses. I was desperately hungry and searching for GOD! I even asked my late first pastor Bishop Robert L. Little if I may get baptized again. When I first got baptized in JESUS's name, some other young people dared me, and I did not want to seem chicken so I did it! They did not know GOD was in all of that even the dare! I wanted to get baptized again because I really wanted this authentic and passionate relationship with GOD for myself!

*For I bear them record that they have
a zeal of God, but not according to
knowledge. (Romans 10:2 KJV)*

As I referenced in my first book *TURNING FROM… TURNING TO…: MY TURNING POINT*, this year in 2021, I reached my thirty-year birthday in CHRIST JESUS! Growing up in church, GOD gave me much exuberance, enthusiasm, and much excitement from Him, but this year of my TURNING POINT! WOW! How GOD has revealed and spoken to me this year alone. I'm telling you, this is truly my new beginning! When this book is released in 2022, I would have circumference in so many new spaces and places.

On November 28, 2021, my pastor Suffragan Bishop Michael Ford Jr. preached a sermon "Chosen Vessels!" To this day, I still watch this sermon on YouTube three to five times at a time of how the POWER of GOD sat on me in this service. GOD has always told me He has chosen me.

> *Ye have not chosen, me, but I have*
> *chosen you, and ordained you, that*
> *ye should go… (John 15:16 KJV)*

This is the exact verse, and again, I was not appreciating GOD as I should. But GOD! I thank GOD for this Sunday, and this sermon, I just sat in church while the pastor was preaching and just crying like, "Oh, my GOD! GOD is talking straight to me through this sermon!" The pastor asked whoever he was talking to come down to the altar. I did not hesitate! Upon arriving at the altar, he was speaking, and the last thing I heard was telling GOD, "I know I messed up, and forgive me, GOD!" At that moment, everything was zoned out. It was just GOD and me. The POWER of GOD sat on me to restore, refresh, rejuvenate, re-anoint, redirect, resolidify, and so much more!

I'd seen no one or heard anything after that! Wow! I had to go back and watch the services, and I still do! GOD did it again! HE had MERCY on little ole me! A piece of dust, made from dirt, but God thought enough to love on me again!

When I had my book signing on December 4, 2021, for my first book, the night before felt as if I was preparing and getting ready for my wedding day! I had gone and got a pedicure and had a hair appointment and had a to-do list to get completed for my big day! On the day of my book signing, GOD dropped in my spirit and a pivotal thought, *I am marrying my PURPOSE!* I am sitting and typing like you had only needed to be there! All the people who came and supported me were crying tears of joy and excitement, sowing seeds, sending and giving me money because they stated they believed in me and are excited about my future!

In a month and a half, I sold over two hundred books. I had people calling and asking if I had more books on me. I just reordered some. I will make sure that I don't run out again. The excitement, zeal, and passion about MY TURNING POINT, I am taking them all over the world. I always keep my books on me and introduce it to everyone that I meet in grocery stores, malls, gas stations, churches, literally everywhere. I say PURPOSE and PASSION have been BIRTHED! I am loving this place, and I will say I HAVE ARRIVED at one of my GOD-given DESTINIES!

I am so encouraged and empowered by what the new year is bringing! Your PASSION should not only be an exciting, empowering, exhilarating, encouraging, and equipping place for you; but it should bless everyone around you to whom it is supposed to bless! I am convinced that some people do not know how to accept or know when there is a blessing in their midst. KING JESUS said it like this.

> **But Jesus said unto them, A prophet is not**
> **without honour, but in his own country, and**
> **among his own kin, and in his own house.**
> **(Mark 6:4 KJV)**

So the scripture above references that your family, friend, foe, and even some church folk may not receive and honor you! You got to keep it movin' and know that there is a huge world out there that is waiting on you to arrive at your DESTINY, PURPOSE, and with much PASSION! So it's not whether people clap for you! Believe in GOD for the impossible and unthinkable. Know that GOD and His heavenly host are cheering you on into the DIVINE PURPOSE with PASSION He has ordained! So do what you love and LOVE what you do, and do it with much PASSION!

MY PAIN BIRTHED MY PURPOSE & MY PASSION!

Snapped Out of It

Throughout life, until we leave this world and go into eternity to stand before KING JESUS, we will have to overcome obstacles that we must SNAP OUT of! We cannot escape some pains (the unexpected), turbulences, highs, and lows; but GOD will get us to the point where we SNAPPED out of IT!

SNAPPED OUT OF WHAT? YOU MAY ASK? EXAMPLES ARE THE FOLLOWING:

- SNAPPED OUT OF NOT MAKING GOD A PRIORITY
- SNAPPED OUT OF MAKING PEOPLE A PRIORITY
- SNAPPED OUT OF ANGER
- SNAPPED OUT OF THINGS OF THE PAST
- SNAPPED OUT OF GUILT
- SNAPPED OUT OF SHAME
- SNAPPED OUT OF DISCOURAGEMENT
- SNAPPED OUT OF FEAR
- SNAPPED OUT OF PEOPLE-PLEASING
- SNAPPED OUT OF SELF-DOUBT
- SNAPPED OUT OF DEPRESSION
- SNAPPED OUT OF BEING LIED TO
- SNAPPED OUT OF BEING A DOORMAT
- SNAPPED OUT OF GIVING PEOPLE PASSES
- SNAPPED OUT OF BEING ANYTHING LESS THAN WHO GOD MADE YOU
- SNAPPED OUT OF BEING ABUSED
- SNAPPED OUT BEING CONFUSED
- SNAPPED OUT OF ASKING WHY
- SNAPPED OUT OF EXPLAINING YOURSELF

- Snapped out of trying to control things that are out of your control
- Snapped out of being a convenience
- Snapped out of being secondary
- Snapped out of being blind to the truth
- Snapped out of being a trash can for garbage
- Snapped out of conforming to what people want or say
- Snapped out of being punked
- Snapped out of being used as a puppet
- snapped out of being a follower
- (now you add to this list)

It is time to snap out of it!

What has pain birthed for you? Ask God, What is supposed to be birthed from this pain?

After nine months of carrying a baby and handling and enduring the pain of birth, something beautiful and majestic is supposed to come forth and be birthed!

What is it that you need to snap out of? Only you can answer these questions.

> *He hath made everything*
> *beautiful in his time:…*
> *(Ecclesiastes 3:11 KJV)*

Let go and let God!
Let go and let purpose flow!
Keep it movin'! My KIM!

> *It's not how you start that's important,*
> *but how you finish. (Jim George)*

I am truly a witness to Jim George's quote above. It is truly not how you start but how you finish! I started this year 2021 a hot mess where I knew better and had the audacity to go against the will of God, but the mercy of God is so rich! I am not finishing this year sloppy like I started but STRONG! GOD has GRACED me to finish this year STRONG! I am truly a MERCY and GRACE child of GOD, and I am heavenly and eternally THANKFUL to GOD for allowing me to find and marry my PURPOSE as an author and to do it with much PASSION!

May the two books that I wrote in one year and one published in the great year of 202WON and this year 2022 (DOUBLE BLESSINGS) bless everyone! I know many have had all types of challenges and losses. I too have faced the unknown in the present and past years, but again, I am a witness that if you TURN FROM self-will and TURN TO GOD's will, you will reach your ultimate TURNING POINT! You too will get to a point and say, as I now declare, "My Pain BIRTHED My PURPOSE & My PASSION!

I SNAPPED OUT of IT!"

GOD BLESS ALL READERS in the name of KING JESUS CHRIST of NAZARETH!

About the Author

QueenDeborah is totally elated, electrified, excited, enriched, enamored, empowered, and equipped for such a time as this! This world needs to be HEALED AND RESTORED and needs to TURN to GOD NOW! QueenDeborah is honored to have felt to write such a book, and she believes it is for NOW!

After a pandemic and all that has happened in the world, it definitely needs to SNAP OUT of IT! What is your IT? Only you and GOD the Creator know! Upon writing this second book, it was the ultimate TURNING POINT for QueenDeborah!

QueenDeborah would go out into the community and share her story and testimony with everyone that she would meet! QueenDeborah believes that this is the time that even JESUS said, … Repent: for the Kingdom of heaven is at hand (Matthew 4:17). QueenDeborah is telling one and all that JESUS is coming, be RAPTURE-ready, because our next seconds is not promised to us!

Before witnessing and ministering, QueenDeborah would always ask GOD to lead her to those who are hungry, seeking, and looking for HIS leading, guidance, help, and hope! There are people hungry for the living GOD, and QueenDeborah, with GOD's help, seeks to find those.

A quote from QueenDeborah's first book, "That what seemed to be the worst of times will and can become the BEST of times!" Let this time be your TIME!

:and who knoweth whether thou art come to the kingdom for such a time as this?

(Esther 4:14 KJV).

QueenDeborah has two degrees from the University of Louisville (Bachelors and Associates), the CEO of LOVING the UNIQUELY YOU, LLC, and enjoys serving and ministering to all that she meets.

QueenDeborah believes it's a blessing to have wealth, but an epiphany that came to her is, "Money does not make us chosen by GOD; it is the ANOINTING and our HEARTS!" Some of the richest people are the most miserable! HEART—h(ear)t-(hear)t = a HEART to have an EAR to HEAR GOD!

Allow this book to minister, heal, help, give hope and all that you need!